"7" THINGS

If I Had Only Known These 7 Things: Timeless Truths and Biblical Wisdom for the Spiritual Journey Ahead

Copyright © 2023 Julie Hicks

All rights reserved.

No part of this publication may be reproduced in a retrieval system, or transmitted in any form or by any means—electronic, mechanical, photocopying, record-ing, or otherwise—without the prior written permission of the publisher.

New International Version® NIV® Copyright © 1973, 1978, 1984, 2011 by Biblica, Inc. TM Used by permission. All rights reserved worldwide. New King James Version (NKJV) English Copyright © 1982 by Thomas Nelson, Inc. Used by permission. All rights reserved.

This manuscript has undergone viable editorial work and proofreading, yet human limitations may have resulted in minor grammatical or syntax-related errors remaining in the finished book. The understanding of the reader is requested in these cases. While precaution has been taken in the preparation of this book, the publisher and author assume no responsibility for errors or omissions, or for damages resulting from the use of the information contained herein.

This book is set in the typeface *Athelas* designed by Veronika Burian and Jose Scaglione.

Paperback ISBN: 979-8-8526-4683-5
Hardcover ISBN: 979-8-8689-3780-4

A Publication of *Tall Pine Books*
119 E Center Street, Suite B4A | Warsaw, Indiana 46580
www.tallpinebooks.com

| 1 23 23 20 16 02 |

Published in the United States of America

(If I had only known these...)

"7" THINGS

*Timeless Truths and Biblical Wisdom
for the Spiritual Journey Ahead*

Julie Hicks

For my Baby

CONTENTS

Foreword *1*
Introduction *5*
Why "7" Things? *7*

"Thing One" *13*
"Thing Two" *21*
"Thing Three" *27*
"Thing Four" *35*
"Thing Five" *43*
"Thing Six" *49*
"Thing Seven" *53*

   "Wrapping It Up" *57*
   Bible Study & Reflection *61*

Special Thanks *99*
About the Author *101*

FOREWORD

A BEAUTIFUL RELATIONSHIP between my sister Julie & I could have been stolen from us had we not plowed through the truths written here. Knowing that we had a common enemy and the same Father desiring victory for us, we slowly grew and moved away from the lies. I testify that the words written here are true. As you sit at your kitchen table, under a big tree, or around a fire and learn seven steps to growing in freedom, you will feel lighter from guilt, more passionate in your calling, and cherished by those God has given you as you cherish them back.

This life is an adventure worth living. I encourage you to make these words part of your story. Don't miss any more of what God has for you. God knew I needed Ms. Julie, and now He's used her to touch you. It may sting, the struggle before you, but trust me, it will be worth it.

These words were prayed over and inspired by not only true events, but through a loving God that used an obedient daughter to author encouragement for you. Get the tissues and get going!

L.B.

INTRODUCTION

(Before reading this section, please see the Bible Study & Reflection for the Introduction)

AS I BEGIN this project, I am writing from my kitchen table...alone. It's funny because for much of my adult life I thought that "alone" would be my preference. But recently, I found myself battling to identify where I belong in this new that life the Lord has led me to. I have basically been alone for the past 2-1/2 years, at least during the week when everyone was off to work and school. We moved to a little town called Parachute in Colorado to be closer to my oldest son. My husband had also found a great job that would better provide for our retirement years and allow him to curb being so tough on his body as a contractor. It all seemed so perfect. But where did I fit in?

Our plan was to find a beautiful home in the mountains to be closer to our oldest son and grandchildren when they came, and for me to start writing (which I had always known I should do). Then, just over a year after us arriving, our oldest son transferred to a new job and moved back to near where we had come from. We looked and looked for the Parachute home of our dreams and ended up "stuck" in a mobile home that we had intended to remodel and flip. We had difficulty finding a new church family to become a part of. I hadn't really found any "friends" to speak of. I was alone. It messed me up. I was so confused. Why had He brought me here for the nothing that I felt like I had? In short, I really felt disappointed in myself, in God, in our situation, in everything.

In the meantime, I had also suffered some very difficult health issues. I have a heart related condition that has progressed and also suffered a near death infection. The list goes on. I kept asking why He was allowing these things in my life. Why was God doing this? Journaling has been one way I cope, so one would think that I would have picked up my pencil (computer as it is today) and started writing some time ago. Instead, I allowed the enemy to control my motivation, intentions, goals, and even God's Will for my life. I neglected to pursue the one thing that my Creator very directly told me to do...write. Doing so led me to feel defeated, lost, afraid, of little consequence, and purposeless. Wait...those are all the exact opposite of who God says I am! Good thing I'm finally getting started. I wouldn't have wanted to believe those things a minute longer. Instead, I am an overcomer, a survivor, found,

Introduction

brave, strong, a tool of the Almighty with an incredible purpose, HIS purpose. My sweet Women's Pastor at Wellspring of Life church here in Parachute reminded me of these things and that I only need to write for Jesus & me. And that, my friends, is why I am writing this book.

Today, I am learning that when I am alone, I can more easily hear His voice. I am surrounded by a wonderful church family that loves and cares for me deeply. I have made a few very dear friends and realized that I can remain connected to the friends I have where we lived previously, many of whom have also moved. My teenage kiddos are doing great in school, my husband is excelling at his job, and I am finally entering into one of the many purposes that He planned for me before I was even born.

My prayer is that as you read these words, you will find the courage to believe in the ultimate love God has for you, discover how he sees you, and continue in or begin to move towards the plan He has for your life. It is good and will give you a hope and a future. ⏰

⏰ Jeremiah 29:11 NIV
11 For I know the plans I have for you," declares the Lord, "plans to prosper you and not to harm you, plans to give you hope and a future.

Anywhere in this text where I refer to myself, please remember to think about how it applies to you in your circumstance. You are not reading this by accident. If you haven't asked Jesus into your heart to be the Lord and Savior of your life and conquer the sin that has ruled over you, do it now...don't wait! When you do, the words written here will make more sense. Enjoy!!

WHY "7" THINGS?
(Before reading this section, please see the Bible Study & Reflection for Why "7" Things?)

IT WAS THE most inquisitive thing when I realized that the Lord had moved me from needing a mentor to being one in certain situations. There were definite people that He appointed to me, and I was so blessed to become a small part of their spiritual journey. To be honest, I always looked at myself as a mess...someone who needed mentoring. As I worked through this, an incredibly wise and lovely sister of mine told me that we are always going to find ourselves in three situations: being encouraged by someone who has been granted wisdom just for us (our mentors & sisters), walking beside someone in a similar place in their spiritual journey (our sisters/brothers), and encouraging someone who needs to be lifted up (being a mentor to others). She was so right. When I started to see this unfold in my own life I was honored and amazed. I, like so many people, asked "Why and how would God use me?" The answer is simple and well explained in God's Word...because He chooses the least to make the greatest difference, that way we can never take the credit. It's always Him when we know we aren't even remotely qualified for the task at hand. Yet there we are, and He's there, too.

> I Corinthians 1:26-31 NKJV
> 26 For you see your calling, brethren, that not many wise according to the flesh, not many mighty, not many noble, are called. 27 But God has chosen the foolish things of the world to put to shame the wise, and God has chosen the weak things of the world to put to shame the things which are mighty; 28 and the base things of the world and the things which are despised God has chosen, and the things which are not, to bring to nothing the things that are, 29 that no flesh should glory in His presence. 30 But of Him you are in Christ Jesus, who became for us wisdom from God—and righteousness and sanctification and redemption- 31 that, as it is written, "He who glories, let him glory in the LORD."

I was so blessed to have been raised in the church and have known Jesus my entire life. Still, I was taught some things that were far from truth, far from grace, and far from how God really sees me. As I began sharing with others what the Lord has done for me, in me and through me, it became apparent that there were some common truths that we all missed at times. I could easily list these truths as the answers to the struggles that I and many people face in receiving God's love in a full and abundant way. They are near and dear to my heart because they were exactly what I needed to understand to begin to move in God's direction for my life. These truths broke the lies that I had believed since I was a child. These truths allowed me to begin to believe that He loves me no matter what, that He would be with me no matter what, that He would carry me when I couldn't get there on my own, and that He would even come for me every time I got lost.

Why "7" Things?

In the past, I got lost a lot. Being a newly dedicated Christian, I felt like I was "trudging" through my life. I wanted to do well but just felt like I failed at it. All in all, it was because my old life was full of hurt, disappointment, self-medication, misunderstanding, and the crazy world I had been living in. I guess I can admit that my "old life" was hard to give up. I was convinced that it was fun, freeing, and even exactly where I wanted to be. Jesus could come with me, but I really didn't want to change my direction.

Then the most amazing thing happened, I figured out God loved me anyway. He loved me right where I was. He was stirring in me a desire to change, a desire to be closer to Him, a desire to leave the hurt behind & grab on to what He had for me. But I didn't have to do all the changing on my own or all at once; I just needed to love Him back, and He would do the changin'. What a relief! I grabbed on to this truth with all I had. I trusted that where I was, He was too. I let Him love me all stinky & gross, and He did.

With this new understanding came a desire to start spending more time with other people who loved Jesus & allowed Him to love them back. I soon found myself surrounded by genuine Christian people who were sharing Jesus' love with me in incredible ways. I suppose most of what I am going to share with you was gleaned from all of them. I will try to give credit where it is due, knowing that it began with my dear brothers & sisters at New Horizon Christian Church in a little town called Dacono, Colorado. As I grew, I encountered others who were where I had been, and I was able to share my newly found faith & understanding. I was able to share how I had figured out that He loves us more than our mistakes, more than our situations, more than anything. He loves us enough to die for us. If I had been the only one that He would have saved, He still would have gone to the cross...just for me!

Even more exciting and important than all of that is the understanding that Jesus dying wasn't the big news. Anyone can do that, and we all will. The big news is that today He's alive! The crucifixion was the beginning, but it was the resurrection that offers the opportunity for us to change the course of our forever by accepting the ultimate gift. Coming alive by God's hand... now that is something only my Savior could do! That is something that only a perfect loving Father could make happen so that every stinky & gross thing that I had ever done or will do, thought or will think, participated in or became a part of was and is washed away. I was made righteous by the blood of Jesus. Because of that, I am now a joint heir to the Kingdom of Heaven and get to look forward to living there for eternity when my time here on earth is done. Whoa! Wait! What? Did you get that? That's big news alright... joint heir with Jesus to the Kingdom of Heaven!! Wow!

I have always enjoyed writing, and at 12 years old I had a poem published in a circulation that was presented at school. I was excited! I recently looked back at that poem and realized that it was not of light and love. I struggled sometimes when I was younger and found writing to be an excellent outlet for my feelings. Although I never considered it to be a possibility for a career, I did continue to write throughout my life. My spiritual journey includes journaling my prayers & feelings, at the suggestion of the same amazing sister I mentioned earlier. It was helpful because it also encouraged me to spend time with the Lord. You can't have a deep friendship if you don't spend quality

Why "7" Things?

time with one another. That is true of any relationship. In short, God had planted a seed of desire for me to write. I have always known it was something He wanted me to do, but writing, knowing someone else would read it, is scary to me. Still, I have always felt this undeniable nudging to get started.

About 10 years ago, I finally started a list of "Books to Write." I wanted to share the most important things that I had come to understand about God's love for me. As I explored it, the first idea on the list was a book sharing the things about God that I wish I'd understood sooner in life. I began to recognize as I spent time with my mentors, sisters, and friends that we all had similar struggles with misunderstandings about God's love for us. It is easy to let the world confuse us about how He sees us, what He wants for us, and how He has made a way for us. He is the creator of all things, including us, and has amazing plans for each of our lives. The truth is that we are worthy of His love through Christ, and He sees us through Jesus' eyes. God is not mad at us, and He will meet us where we are. This life is short (even in struggle) compared to eternity in paradise (where there is no struggle). With obedience comes blessing, and a good Father disciplines His children when they misbehave. God's love is not a feeling but an example of action, and relationship with Him is a real possibility if we spend some time with Him.

In preparing this first project, I made out my "list" of things. These were things that not only changed my life, but also my perspective and true understanding of how BIG my God is. Lo and behold...there were seven things. I should not have been surprised. After all, seven is a favorite number of His and represents completion over and over in His Word. I certainly don't profess to be complete, but when I begin to grasp the depth of His love and allow Him to move in and through my life, then I can begin to experience the peace and rest that comes from trusting a God who is fully in control, fully aware. When I learn to listen for His voice and move when He calls me to, then I can begin to experience His Will in my life. If I fully trust that He is good and knows what is best for me, then I can begin to enjoy contentment in even the most difficult of circumstances.⚓ None of us will be perfect at it until we find ourselves in Heaven, but we can get a great start, "... His Kingdom come, on earth as it is in Heaven.

⚓ Romans 5:1-5 NKJV
1 Therefore, having been justified by faith, we have peace with God through our Lord Jesus Christ 2 through whom also we have access by faith into this grace in which we stand, and rejoice in hope of the glory of God. 3 And not only that, but we also glory in tribulations knowing that tribulation produces perseverance; 4 and perseverance, character; and character, hope. 5 Now hope does not disappoint, because the love of God has been poured out in our hearts by the Holy Spirit who was given to us.

"THING ONE"

(Before reading this section, please see the Bible Study & Reflection for "Thing One.")

GOD IS NOT mad at me, and His love is unconditional! As one of my sisters in Christ reflected, "He's not sitting up in Heaven in front of some computer screen waiting to zap me when I mess up." God is not interested in punishing me for my sins because when I received Jesus Christ as my Lord and Savior, my sin debt was paid in full. Now when He looks at me, He only sees the beautiful & righteous woman that He made me to be. The Bible tells us that Father God passed the authority to judge me and my sins to His Son, Jesus Christ, who was willing to die for it all. So, is Jesus mad at me? I could see where He could be quite disappointed at my decisions at times, but He's not mad either. He is filled with joy at

> John 5:26-27 NKJV
> 26 For as the Father has life in Himself, so He has granted the Son to have life in himself, 27 and has given Him authority to execute judgment also, because He is the Son of Man.

my willingness to receive His gift. And should God the Father have a question about my worthiness to be loved & spoiled by Him, Jesus' reply will always be, "I died for that." My own way of making this real for me is to imagine that when He did, a miraculous "Jesus Screen" of himself was inserted that God the Father looks through when He looks at me. This screen is miraculous and erases every blemish of sin that would be apparent to God without it. Just imagine, when God looks down from Heaven through the "Jesus Screen," all He sees is beautiful. I don't have to dwell in a place of guilt and shame anymore, and I shouldn't, because doing so really means that I don't believe that Jesus' death & resurrection are enough for me. But they are!

I am convinced that this is the most important thing that we can come to understand about God and His love. Without this understanding, we could find ourselves in a burdened spiral for the rest of our lives. No matter who we are, where we come from, what blessings we have experienced, what challenges we face, none of it matters if we don't have a correct understanding of how God looks at us. If we believe in God and we go through life thinking He's mad at us or in any way displeased with our "performance" here on earth, it is going to end up crushing us. When we live in that place, there is no reason for satan to mess with us, because he knows we are doing a fine job being "stuck" all on our own. It's a terrible feeling to think that someone is disappointed in us, or that we've let someone down, especially God. It strains our self-worth and tears down our confidence in trying new ways to use our natural gifts to further His Kingdom. Thinking anyone, but especially the God of the universe, is mad at me

Thing One

made me sad and crazy...and made me want to run away.

I spent a lot of my childhood believing that I had Jesus in my heart, so I was going to Heaven. Yet I still grew up believing that somehow I was bad. I was a bit of a rebellious child and often found myself in situations that required a decision to do right or wrong (of course). I tried so hard but failed to make the best decision more than I'd like to admit. I am not sure why; it just seemed easier to do the wrong thing. Two of my biggest obstacles were wanting to be liked and wanting to be a winner. I remember trying so hard, and yet I was always the "loser." As a small child, I began to cheat at games, cards, contests & the like. Soon I found that no one wanted to play with me anymore. I figured out the hard way that people are more apt to like an honest loser than a cheating winner. It was a hard lesson because even though I figured it out eventually, I ruined a lot of relationships and I missed out on friendships that could have been very meaningful in my life. I carried around the guilt and shame associated with that with me for a very long time...even into adulthood. In doing so, I also bought into the idea that those childhood decisions made me unworthy of God's love and unworthy of others' love, too.

I remember being told that God would be mad at me if I didn't start "behaving myself." I also remember how disappointed my dad was in me because I was always doing or saying the wrong thing. Growing up I was a daddy's girl, so it was awful that he felt that way. I tried with each new day. Still, I found myself on the wrong end of things over and over. My dad's disappointment was more impactful in my early teens than the thought of God being disappointed. I think every teenager goes through a time where they are really asking themselves if what they were taught as a kid is truth, so I really didn't think a whole lot about that. But my love for Jesus always was, and still is, very real and kept me in a battle between right and wrong that prevented me from going off the deep end. Still, I was very burdened by my tendency to do the wrong thing. Soon I had decided that I just wasn't right. If I wanted terribly to do right but still did wrong, why try? So, I didn't. I became more rebellious. Oh, the agony I put my parents through. And all because I thought God was more and more mad at me with every mistake I made. I know that they meant well but telling me that God would be mad at me just wasn't truth and really damaged my self-worth.

> Romans 7:15 NKJV
> 15 I do not understand what I do. For what I want to do I do not do, but what I hate I do.

As a young adult, I found myself in situations where my first choice was to do anything that would take me away from the reality that I had disappointed everyone growing up. My family is prone to addiction, and I am no exception. I began to drink and experiment with drugs in my early 20s. Again, knowing Jesus as my Savior kept me from going further than I could find my way back from, but that was still pretty far. Being drunk or stoned seemed great. I didn't have to think about doing the right thing, or the thousands of times that I already had not. People at the bar liked me and we had a great time every time I was there. There was no judgment because we were all doing the same thing. I could dance, sing, and just let my real life go. The only problem was that I had to wake up the next day and grab back onto my reality.

Nothing changed, and because I knew my lifestyle was

wrong, my desire to escape grew. It became a vicious cycle of wanting to escape, despising the choices I made, believing God was mad at me, trying to do better, not being able to, and yearning to be different because of His love. Eventually, I began to think that I couldn't even look for Him until I got "right." The world is full of people who believe the very same thing...you have to clean up first, then you can come to God. But that's like taking a shower after you put your clothes on.

By the time I was in my late 20s/early 30s, I was generally back in a church pew again on Sunday mornings. I was trying so hard to figure it out. Yet, I always felt like I just shouldn't be there given what I had done the night before. Relationships came and went during this time. I compromised myself as a mother, daughter, sister, friend, and woman. I was trudging through life and carrying a lot of baggage; my choices, my disappointments, others' disappointments in me, all of it. It was fair to say that I was even a little torqued at God. I mean, the folks at the church I grew up in said that if I was good and asked, He would help me. Oh, I tried...and...tried and asked...and asked, and it felt like no help came. But I was not so much asking for help but rather asking for Him to condone my behavior so I could feel better about the terrible choices I was making. I mean I wasn't hurting anyone but myself. Looking back, I know that this statement was such a lie from the enemy, and it worked to keep me right where I was for the longest time: Stuck, trapped, afraid, sad, disappointed, frustrated, and addicted. Yet I still knew the answer was in Jesus.

I started attending Bible study and spending more and more time in God's Word. I also started praying more purposefully and more frequently; for others and in praise & worship, instead of for myself. I was experiencing something that went like this...praise Him where you are, and He will make the desire to change come alive in you. It seemed odd to me that I really wanted to be different. I had always really enjoyed being in the bar. But I began to desire change in my life. Not so much for me, but so that people could see God in me. I was beginning to think about how my actions and behaviors reflected on what other people thought about God. Trust me, up until this point, I lied to myself every day by saying I didn't care what other people thought. The truth was that I needed to acknowledge, for the first time in my adult life, how my actions affected others, and how they saw or didn't see God through me and how I was living my life. Not so long after all of this, I heard somewhere that following Jesus and walking in His Grace was not a "free to sin card," it was a "sin free card." Paul said it best in Romans 6:1-2. Yikes, talk about conviction!

I remember telling my Pastor at the time that I felt like I had missed my calling; that I had already missed my opportunity to serve God with my time, talents, and treasures. He simply replied, "You can't miss God." I had already wasted so much of my adult life serving myself. It was at this point that I was beginning to fully understand that I shouldn't get dressed before I showered; I would get cleaner if I just let God meet me where I was. Then the most amazing thing began to happen...I started seeing God where I was. He was there, and He wasn't mad at me! I'm not condon-

☂ Romans 6:1-2 NKJV
1 What shall we say, then? Shall we go on sinning so that grace may increase? 2 By no means! We are those who have died to sin; how can we live in it any longer?

Thing One

ing where I was or what I was doing, but I remember being so excited that even at the bar (I was still drinking), God was with me. I started telling all my drinking buddies about Jesus and how He loved us all. So much so that most of them wanted me to just "hush it." Conviction does hurt at times. 😉

Something else that was beginning to make sense as I realized God was not mad at me was that Jesus died on the cross some 2000+ years ago, long before I was born. So, I contemplated, "How many of my present-day sins were ones that I would commit in the future from the day Christ died on the cross to pay my debt for them?" Right, you got it...all of them! Jesus went to the cross for every sin that I would commit from the day I was born forward. He is fully aware of my future and the decisions I will make along the way, and yet He did it anyway. He has already paid the debt for what I have done and what I will do long before I did any of it. God doesn't run by our clock. Jesus agreed to bear all that sin, all that shame, all that disappointment, all that chaos, all that tragedy, all that illness, all of it. When I fail to recognize that, it is not much different than punching Him in the gut. When I fail to operate in this incredible gift, it's like telling Him, "Thanks anyway." Can you imagine His broken heart as Jesus thinks, and maybe even calls out loud, "But I laid down my life for you?"

We are human and not capable of being perfect...only God is capable of that. I know that I am going to make mistakes, even given that I have come to know Jesus as my Savior. But He has given me the instruction (His Word) and opportunity (His Will) to tap into His amazing grace & mercy for each "oops" I find myself sorry for. There is still a process for receiving this grace & mercy, and it starts with knowing that I have messed up. Next is finding it in my heart to want to be different; to want not to do it again. Then I just turn AWAY from what I have done and turn TO Jesus. I let Him know that I want to be free from my sin, that I want to walk away from the trudging & start moving in the freedom that comes from knowing I am forgiven. It is a beautiful place to be, so beautiful. God is not mad at me...thank you Jesus!

"THING TWO"

(Before reading this section, please see the Bible Study & Reflection for "Thing Two.")

THIS LIFE IS short and temporary by God's design. When I was a small child, 35 to 40 years old seemed ancient. If someone made it to 60 years old, they were definitely standing with one foot in the grave (hee hee). Time is such a fleeting and yet lasting thing. But when I compare this life with eternity, forever, never ending, continuing indefinitely, an infinite existence in paradise…well then, no matter how long I live here, it is just a moment. The Bible tells us that "Man is like a breath. His days are like a passing shadow." Psalm 144:4 NKJV.

I believe it was during a retreat early in my walk when a speaker showed us something that helped me understand how quickly this life passes. She took a very long piece of thread…maybe 15 ft. or so. She then colored the teeny tiny tip of the thread with a black marker. As they stretched the thread across the room, the white portion was intended to represent eternity and the black portion was intended to represent our time in this life. It made so much sense. And if I could imagine that there was no end to the white portion, then I could see the possibility and importance of being able to exist in this life with joy through anything. It sounds so simple, I know. It is equally difficult to accomplish, I know. But, when we feed our souls with what God has offered, His Word, His Son, His Spirit, His Love, His Vision, His Purpose, then we can truly see that His intentions for each of us are pure and full of hope for eternity. ⏰ If I can wrap my head around this, it allows me to rest in my circumstances, no matter what they are. I do not profess to have mastered this; I am often wallowing in self-pity for a time until He reminds me. But I find myself coming back much more quickly the more time I spend with God.

> ⏰ Jeremiah 29:11 NKJV
> 11 For I know the plans I have for you," declares the Lord, "plans to prosper you and not to harm you, plans to give you hope and a future.

I frequently describe this to others as the "Jesus Train." I can't remember where I got this, but I think I came up with it on my own. If you are reading this and it was your metaphor, my apologies. Anyway...as I said before, I grew up in the church and have always known Jesus. As a small child, I rode the Jesus Train gladly and never got off. In my early teens, I began to jump off the train on occasion and wander off a ways. Into my late 20s, I was jumping off and running a town or two away. Sometimes, I even found myself in the next state. It was such a long, hard journey back to the station. As I began to spend more time with

Thing Two

God and in His Word, I found myself understanding the long haul of getting back to where I had jumped off the train. It was like starting over in a sense. I could have been using the time and energy moving forward in God's plan for my life instead of trudging back to the station. So over time, I was jumping off the train less frequently, and when I did, I wasn't going quite so far. Now there are even times when I just touch my big toe on the ground below the train and pull it right back in. I don't want to get off the Train, I want to ride it forever. Still, the temptations of this world pull on me..."Come on, just jump off for a moment." It is with great delight that I can now most often say, "No." Then I turn and look into the face of my Savior and know that the train I'm on is going in the right direction and headed exactly where He wants me to go. If I do find myself on the ground next the train, I can simply reach up and grab His hand and He pulls me back in. Thank you Jesus!

In this lifetime, I face some difficult health issues, tough relationship issues, personality issues, temptations, and times when I give in to them, and your everyday, "Why am I here and what am I supposed to be doing?" struggles. It is so easy to find myself looking at this life as "long" because of the struggles. As I enter my "years of wisdom" (we'll call them that), it is also easy to look back and desire that I had done things differently. Why didn't I accomplish more, make more sense of God's calling for my life? Why wasn't I more proactive about sharing the gospel? Why didn't I encourage my children differently so that all these things were solidified in them, so they wouldn't have to wrestle them, too? But then ever so gently the Holy Spirit reminds me of all that I've written here, and I remember that one day there will be no more struggle. One day, I will gain an understanding (along with everyone else who calls Jesus their Savior) of why all this struggle had to take place and the beauty that resulted from it, and all will be well forever.

It is with a sincere heart that I encourage you to pray over these things. We all face incredible hardships in this life. We will all suffer loss. We will all suffer condemnation. We will all face criticism. We will be tempted and tricked by the enemy and participate in things we will regret. There will be times when tomorrow seems so far away, when yesterday won't let us go, when today is just too heavy to carry. These are the times when we need this knowledge. If we can remind ourselves that this life is so short and forever in paradise is what is to come, then we can learn to lay down our sorrows at the feet of Jesus and move forward in our circumstances, knowing that they will not last forever.

I believe there is a difference between joy and happiness. Happiness is circumstantial, but the Joy of the Lord is a gift. There is nothing more precious than realizing that we are not alone in this journey and that this life is meant as a gift, too. As we learn to hold on to this truth, the struggles we face become less impactful and more manageable. If everything were always wonderful, why would we need a Savior? It is so important to realize that when we are in the fire, we are being refined by the One True God who loves us and wants us to be our very best for Him when we do get to eternity. We are part of an incredible army being groomed and raised in this life to accomplish

🔥 Isaiah 48:19 NKJV
19 Behold, I have *refined* you, but not as silver; I have tested you in the furnace of affliction

Thing Two

what God has set before us in the next. As a child of the One True King, we should be appreciative of the way He loves, disciplines, instructs, trains, and rescues us in the short time we are here. He wants what is best for me and you. The choices we make are His to work for the good. It may not look or feel good to us, we just have to believe that it is. We will not be here long and will soon find ourselves in the presence of a God who planned it all perfectly. Indeed, this life is short and temporary, and eternity in paradise is what is to come for those who have allowed Jesus Christ into their hearts and acknowledged Him as their Lord and Savior.

Romans 8:28 NIV
And we know that *in* all things God works for the good of those who love him, who have been called according to His purpose.

"THING THREE"

(Before reading this section, please see the Bible Study & Reflection for "Thing Three.")

I CAN TAKE the hard road or the easy road. Now we've established that this life is short, so do I want to spend it struggling? I have seen so many people who are moving through this life with so much difficulty, including myself at times. Life's circumstances are so tough that sometimes all we feel we are doing is putting one foot in front of the other and ending up some place we really don't want to be. I've been there over and over, and always found myself asking how I got to where I was. The answer is really simple...in a lot of cases, I was making horrible choices.

It will be impossible for me to make the right choice all the time, but when I do, God rejoices with me. We are all born into sin; what Adam and Eve did make this true. Even a small child knows how to lie without being taught, so I don't need to be hard on myself (or others) for being realistic about this. I don't have to be looking over my shoulder wondering when I am going to get caught. God already knows it's coming. I am going to make mistakes, even as I get to know God more intimately. My greatest prayer is that my mistakes become smaller and less frequent, and they have. God sees this and He oozes with joy at my willingness to draw near to Him. And like a good parent, He will reward me for my willingness to listen. I can be sure that my Heavenly Father is looking at me in love and is so proud of me for trying, even though I'm not perfect.

It's hard to remember, amid the fun this world seems to offer, that this life really is short and temporary. Something may be fun for the moment but may be harmful to me and devastating to those who love me. The destructive behavior that I demonstrated got in the way of the beautiful plan God had for my life. I was wasting precious time that I could have spent growing closer to Him. I was wasting time that I could have used to serve others, time I could have spent sharing the good news that Jesus was willing to give up His presence in paradise to come to this, um, "interesting" place. He was willing to live a life in which most people opposed everything that He was sent to share and do. He knew he would be beaten until He was unrecognizable and be slain in the most humiliating way on a Roman cross. He was willing to do all of this just so that He could get to the part where He was raised from the dead. He now sits at the right hand of God the Father in Heaven, interceding on our behalf. His sole purpose in doing all of this was to give us the opportunity to spend

Thing Three

eternity with Him. He did it for me and for you! Oh my, I was wasting time!

Because He loves me so much, because He doesn't want me to waste time, and because He especially wants me to move in and enjoy the plan He has for my life, He disciplines when I act out. But what does that mean exactly? What I have come to understand in my own life is that weird struggles often arise when I'm not "behaving" by making choices that I know aren't what God wants for me. Not that we don't all have struggles, we do. And just because we have a struggle doesn't mean we are acting out. God was very clear to make sure we understood that this life will have struggles. But He was also very good in that He was intentional to remind us that He is always with us as we make our way through them. Those aren't the struggles I am talking about though; they are more the struggles that occur when I make choices that I know aren't the "right" ones, the struggles that occur when I have jumped off the Jesus train and gotten lost, the struggles that I could have avoided if I had just turned to Him and asked Him if it was okay. He will always give me the right answer.

> John 16:33 NIV
> 33 "I have told you these things, so that *in* me you may have peace. *In this world* you will have trouble. But take heart! I have overcome the *world*."

With disobedience comes discipline. You'll see that I seem to know a little more about this than the obedience part to come. It is true, and I am ever so thankful that I wasn't forgotten or loved less for my choices. I was picked up, brushed off, encouraged, and sent on my way with God's hope that I would do it different next time, and the next, and the next.... He chose to refine me instead of giving up on me. Thank you, Lord! He chose to believe in my tomorrow when all I was doing was wasting my today. Thank you, Lord! He chose to see what He made me to be, instead of how I was operating in the world. Thank you, Lord! He chose to parent me with love and discipline to reveal how much better and easier it could be if I only chose to follow Him. A great parent is always interested in the direction their child is going. The most incredible thing about being a child of God is that not only is He interested in the direction I am going, but He already knows what will happen when I get there (wherever that may be). It is His pleasure and desire to guide me along the way. And yes, to get my attention, He may need to discipline my actions so that I know that He is serious about the fact that I am going THE WRONG WAY!

> Matthew 7:13-14 NIV
> 13 "Enter through the narrow gate. For wide is the gate and broad is the road that leads to destruction, and many enter through it. 14 But small is the gate and narrow the road that leads to life, and only a few find it."

Likewise, with obedience comes blessings and freedom! When I am making good choices, spending time in the Word of God, spending time in prayer, and spending time serving others, then I am free. You just can't feel guilt, shame, disappointment, misunderstanding, and the like in the presence of God. His love covers them all. Instead, my time with Christ is spent recognizing and acknowledging God's presence and plan in my life. I can walk knowing that He's got me, that what He is doing is good. I can acknowledge that He is opening and closing doors to continually keep me moving toward Him, though I may at times take a detour. There is no greater peace than knowing that the Creator of the Universe is walking with me every step I take, that He is watching every step I take and guiding me to the right path. Indeed, it is narrow, but the rewards should be enough to push forward between its boundaries for a lifetime. I'm not so great with boundaries, but He brings me back.

Thing Three

I know that I can look to God for wisdom, counseling, healing, guidance, knowledge, understanding, sustenance, and any other need I may have in this life. I seem to turn to Him most often when I need something. God is really okay with that. He'll take whatever time I am willing to give to Him. But He desires something so much more personal and intimate. He desires relationship with me, and we'll discover more about this in Thing Four. For now, let me just say that the depth of His love for us is unlimited and never ending. He always wants what is best for me, so it's important to remember that if He is a good Father (and He most certainly is), then I can count on Him to redirect my path when I am going the wrong direction.

Think of a parent who loves their children and wants what is best for them. They would gladly give up their own needs for the needs of their child. When a child misbehaves or does something dangerous, the parent does their best to redirect the child and offer discipline for the offense. A good parent always operates out of a desire to aid their child in making a better choice next time, never out of anger. Equally, a good parent forgives and doesn't stay mad, but they still discipline. God calls this "Grace." He offers it freely to me, and I get as many "do overs" as I need. His grace is enough for each and every offense that I commit, and I never have to worry if His love for me has changed. It hasn't! I'm so thankful that no matter what, He loves me the same.

God is our model for parenting. One of God's most endearing names is "Abba," or "Daddy/Father." He is the best Father we can ask for. His correction is with love, and His grace is never ending. But He will not allow us to continually be destructive and cruel to ourselves or

---

Hebrews 12:5-6 NKJV
5 And have you forgotten the exhortation which speaks to you as to sons: "My son, do not make light of the Lord's discipline, and do not lose heart when he rebukes you, because the Lord disciplines the one He loves, and He chastens everyone he accepts as His son."

Psalm 30:5 NKJV
5 "For His anger is but for a moment, His favor is for a life; Weeping may endure for a night, but joy comes in the morning.

others without consequence. If we continually make this our choice, we will struggle. We will be traveling the hard road of captivity and pain. It may be fun in the moment, but the regret will build, and one day it will be more than we can bear. That sounds like horrible news, but it isn't. When things are more than we can bear, that is when we can clearly see our need for a Savior. He wants to carry it all and He wants us to rely on Him to do it.

Some people call it a conscience. The Webster's Dictionary defines "conscience" as "an inner feeling or voice viewed as acting as a guide to the rightness or wrongness of one's behavior." That definition so directly describes the Holy Spirit. He has come to live inside of everyone who has asked Jesus into their hearts. He lives inside of me and is always available to guide me when I'm not sure what direction I should go or what I should do. The thing is, He's not really a screamer though. His voice is described once in the Bible as a "...still small voice" that came after the wind, earthquake, and fire. The significance is that God is not constrained to one mode of communication. It is not always loud like thunder. The Holy Spirit is more of a gentleman and most often waits for me to realize that I need His help. Unfortunately, I basically need someone to hit me over the head with a 2x4 if they want to get my attention. My usual "mode of operation" is thinking that I don't need help; I can do it on my own. Oh, how that attitude has caused me so much heartache and pain. I do need

> 1 King 19:11-12 NKJV
> 11 Then He said, "Go out, and stand on the mountain before the LORD." And behold, the LORD passed by, and a great and strong wind tore into the mountains and broke the rocks in pieces before the LORD, *but* the LORD *was* not in the wind; and after the wind an earthquake, *but* the LORD *was* not in the earthquake; 12 and after the earthquake a fire, *but* the LORD *was* not in the fire; and after the fire a still small voice.

help, I do need direction, I do need love, I do need others, and I do need Jesus! Being able to say that has brought me more peace in my life than I can describe. I have finally come to the point where I just don't want to trudge anymore. I don't want to struggle because of the crappy decisions I have made. I want to be free.

Those in the world who are citizens of the world (by the way – I am not, I'm a citizen of Heaven☺) will often say that the "Jesus Way" is too restrictive and harsh, but what it actually offers is freedom and peace. It comes in a less conspicuous way and is on the inside more than the outside. It has more to do with our own peace and joy and is more about serving God and others than serving ourselves and our own desires. If I live being more concerned about what someone else needs than what I want, it rarely goes wrong. 👍 With the guidance of the Holy Spirit, I can make the right choices and the road I travel is more like a smooth, paved highway…which is so much easier to navigate than a deeply rutted dirt road.

☺ Ephesians 2:19 NKJV
19 Now, therefore, you are no longer strangers and foreigners, but fellow citizens with the saints and members of the household of God,…

👍 Philippians 2:3 NKJV
Let nothing be done through selfish ambition or conceit, but in lowliness of mind let each esteem others better than himself.

"THING FOUR"

(Before reading this section, please see the Bible Study & Reflection for "Thing Four.")

RELATIONSHIP WITH GOD is tangible and real. My God is not absent, He is ever present in my life. The greatest purpose that I have is the reason God made me... to Love Him. And because I do, I choose to do my best to follow Him. I'm so thankful that when Jesus called His first disciples, when He said, "Put down your nets and follow me," they answered, "Yes." How different things could have been if even one of them had said "No." They did not. How different things would have been if Jesus had said "No." He did not. And because of that, I now have access to the knowledge and wisdom that offers the beautiful opportunity for me to walk with Him side by side.

One important tidbit in my understanding of "Thing Four" is that in ancient times, before Jesus came to die for our sins, only the High Priest could enter into God's

> **Mark 15:38 NKJV**
> 37 And Jesus cried out with a loud voice, and breathed His last. 38 Then the veil of the temple was torn in two from top to bottom.

> **Hebrews 4:16 NKJV**
> 16 Let us therefore come boldly to the throne of grace, that we may obtain mercy and find grace to help in time of need.

> **Colossians 4:2 NKJV**
> 2 Devote yourselves to prayer with an alert mind and a thankful heart.

presence and appeal on the people's behalf for the forgiveness of their sins, for the request for provision, for any reason. To do so, he would enter a chamber in the temple through a large, heavy curtain that hung from ceiling to floor. The Bible tells us that when Jesus breathed His last, the veil was torn from top to bottom. No longer was there anything between God and His people whom He loves deeply. I can approach the throne with confidence, crawl up on His lap, and let Him put His arms around me while I have a good cry, hang out with Him and tell Him about my day, apologize when I fall, thank Him when He forgives, all of it...in His presence. What an awesome gift, to be able to spend one on one time with the One who created me.

No matter how God chooses to communicate with me, it will be impossible for me to hear if I am constantly talking over Him. If I want to hear Him as we spend time together, I have to be willing to be quiet and listen. His voice is soothing, gentle, beautiful, and full of wisdom. But if I am to have a conversation with God, I have to stop talking some of the time. Now, don't get me wrong--prayer (us talking to God) is something He has asked us to participate in with dedication and thanksgiving. But if all I do is talk TO Him, and even AT Him, then I can't hear His response. God's voice will come from inside (the Holy Spirit in me), from His Word, from the words of others whom He has inspired on my behalf, and maybe from somewhere I can't

Thing Four

even see. But no matter where it comes from, I won't be able to hear it if I'm so enamored with my own voice that I don't want to "shut it" sometimes. Relationship is always more about listening than talking, it just is.

I'll never forget the first time I heard God say my name. I was singing in the praise group at that small church in Dacono, Colorado. We often sang this song that talked about "when He called my name." I can't even remember what song it was; I'll have to research that. But anyway, I kept telling myself, "Yeah right, I've never heard Him call my name." Then, as I grew in my faith, I started praying and asking God to allow me to hear Him say it. One day, on that very stage, He did. It was as audible as I can describe. "Julie," He said. As you can imagine, I didn't do a whole lot of singing after that, but instead a lot of thankful crying. Is that a thing? Yes, most definitely. I've done it many times since. All this to say He is here, He is real, and He is very much at work in the lives of every one of us, including me.

If I want to grasp how this relationship is tangible (perceptible by touch), I must understand that God's Word, the Holy Bible, is alive. I can pick it up, feel it, turn the pages, read it, and He will surely speak to me through it. If you have read a verse or text in the Bible on more than one occasion, you may have noticed that one time you will understand "this," and the next time from the same text you will understand "that." Through His Word that lives, He reveals to us what we need each time we seek Him through it. I can't pick and choose what parts and pieces of the Bible I believe to be true because the Bible, in its entirety, is what God has given me as my "instruction manual." I always say, "IF Before all else fails, read the

---

Hebrews 4:12 NKJV
12 For the Word of God is living and powerful, and sharper than any two-edged sword, piercing even to the division of the soul and spirit, and of joints and marrow, and is a discerner of the thoughts and intents of the heart.

I Peter 1:23 NKJV
23 having been born again, not of corruptible seed but incorruptible, through the Word of God which lives and abides forever.

instructions." When I read it, God is speaking directly to me through His Word.

In trying to completely understand who God is and how He loves me and wants to spend time with me, my imagination sees that He spends a good amount of time chasing me down or following me around. Yikes! Imagine turning my back on and walking away from God. That's ugly. I know this for sure: it is never God who walks away, so if I'm feeling distant from Him, it is me who has turned the other direction. But He will always follow. He will never leave or forsake me. Not only is God the Father watching over me, God the Son is walking with me, and God the Holy Spirit is living within me to be my guide when I am willing to let Him do so. That's a lot of super amazing God stuff going on in my life, and all because He wants to spend time with me.

I used to think that if God the Father, Son and Holy Spirit are doing all of that, why do I need to do anything? The answer is simple: because He tells me to, and relationship is never one-sided, it takes two. Think of your best friendship and how it would be if you had only met once or twice and then never saw each other or talked with each other again. Would it still be your best friendship today? The answer is no. It takes spending time with a person, getting to know them, sharing in their hopes, dreams, desires, struggles, and lives before you can call it a close relationship. When those things are absent, then we can still call it a relationship, but it will be more accurately described as an acquaintance, strained, distant,

> Hebrews 13:5 NKJV
> 5 Let your conduct be without covetousness; be content with such things as you have. For He Himself has said, "I will never leave you nor forsake you."

and/or superficial. That is not the relationship God wants with me.

God is the perfect Father, and when I started out in this whole relationship thing, I was more like the rebellious teenager. I implied with my actions that He wasn't very smart; that He didn't really know what was best for my life; that God really didn't need to interfere with what I had going on; that His discipline would be better spent on someone who didn't have it all together like I did. If you have been through the teenage years with a child, you know exactly what I'm talking about.

As parents, we do our best to be patient in these times, though it certainly isn't always easy. We pray that our kiddos will get it one day. It may be one day soon, or it may take a lifetime, but we pray they will get it. We can also assume that life won't be easy for them as they go through the process of figuring it out. We know that with disobedience comes consequences, so we pray that God will protect them as they make decisions that may have a negative impact on their futures. Then we hope that we've parented them well enough that they'll find their way to the amazing future God has for them, even with all our imperfections. We look forward to celebrating with them, even with all the mistakes we've made along the way. Thankfully, God – our perfect daddy – doesn't make mistakes, EVER! Now that I'm paying attention, I can see He's "raising me" right and watching for me to turn to Him.

I can so easily look back on my life and see the times I have struggled and see that I wasn't hanging out with God much. I can just as easily look back and see the times when I have been most at peace and able to manage the challenges that arose and recognize that I was walking with Him. It is the times when I am in His Word regularly, on my knees often, and sharing His light and love with others that my focus is less on me and more on Him. And that is when I can allow Him to move me instead of trying to do everything on my own. It is never wrong when God is in charge. That isn't to say that it's easy. As I said before, He was sure to tell us not to fear the difficulties of the world because we WILL have them. But He also reminded us that He has overcome the world, so we don't need to fret about what comes our way. Whether we allow Him to or not, He's walking WITH us through all of it...the great, the good, the hard, the bad, the sorrow, the celebration-all of it. He is with me! And because He is with me, I can even count my trials as joy.

Why would we need a Savior, if not for the struggles, for the difficulties, for the brokenness, for the undesirable situations? If everything were great all the time, why would we turn to Him? Sometimes He has to let the hardship in so we can fall on our knees and ask Him for help. But this is different than asking Him for "stuff." I know that God rejoices when I remember to thank Him first, but I sometimes forgot this part early in my journey. Mostly, I recall asking Him for what I thought would make my life more perfect, more manageable, more agreeable, more in line with what I expected in my future. As I have grown in seeing Him through "thankful lenses" and recognizing the blessings that He showers-- and I mean showers--on me every day, I

> James 1:2-4 NKJV
> 2 My brethren, count it all joy when you fall into various trials, 3 knowing that the testing of your faith produces patience. 4 But let patience have its perfect work, that you may be perfect and complete, lacking nothing.

Thing Four

am learning to ask less for me and more for everyone else. God loves that!

You see, serving others is the only thing that Jesus came to do. If I want to be more like Him, I have to start there. I can't start there if I'm not spending time with the one TRUE God who planned it all. Again, I don't profess to having perfected this, only that I understand the importance of spending time with the most important Being I will ever have the awesome opportunity to get to know. And when I do spend that time with God, everything else goes better. He knows the secret desires of my heart. Don't think for a moment that they aren't important to Him. They are...He told me so. ♥

♥ Psalm 37:4 NKJV
4 Take delight in the Lord, and he will give you the desires of your heart.

"THING FIVE"

(Before reading this section, please see the Bible Study & Reflection for "Thing Five.")

TRUE LOVE IS not a feeling, it's an action. Sometimes the most difficult thing we will ever "do" is love someone. The only way to love properly is to follow God's example and give selflessly. Wow, that's a mouthful and a huge life calling. But God didn't just say, "Yada, yada, yada, and by the way, I love you;" instead, He showed me what it meant. He prayed, gave, did, said, came, went, fed, moved, washed, cried, rebuked, taught, rejoiced, and more. He continues to "do" so today. His words are never empty; He follows them up with action, and I am to do the same. 🔒 Just the fact that God's Word is "written" shows action. He loves perfectly by doing, not just saying.

How do you know someone loves you? Is it because they tell you they do, or is it because of the way they "act" towards you? What I mean is if I tell someone I love them

> 🔒 I John 4:10-11 NKJV
> 10 In this is love, not that we loved God, but that He loved us and sent His Son to be the propitiation for our sins. 11 Beloved, if God so loved us, we also ought to love one another.

but then treat them horribly all the time, do you think they believe me? Probably not. Unfortunately, and most often, we are hardest on the people God has given us to love the most, and that love us the most back. It seems safer to be mean to someone I know is going to take it without walking away from me than someone I barely know and could care little about. Oddly, I could turn it on and off like a switch when someone from church walked in and then back out. I've really damaged some of my most cherished relationships by thinking love was only a feeling and that I didn't have to follow it up with my actions. How horrible I have been at times to those I "love."

Unfortunately, I spent a good portion of my late 20s and early 30s drinking way too much. When I drink too much, the only person I am thinking about is me. I'm pretty sure satan designed it this way to keep us from loving each other. I fail miserably at love when I'm not in my right mind, and I hurt others in the process. Alcohol removes my ability to love with action. Part of my learning to love with action meant giving up on the things that prevent me from doing so. Occasionally--twice in the last 7 years--I have tested the theory that I can now handle drinking abundantly and should be okay. Not so! I'm still incredibly stupid when I drink and am unable to love even the most lovable in my life. Sometimes loving with action is changing me so I can think clearly enough about what someone else needs, and then love them by being a part of it. I'm still learning!

There isn't some big secret to loving properly. The more I understand the way Jesus loves, the more I realize it doesn't have to be a grand, perfect gesture. The most heartfelt reactions can come from the smallest of whis-

Thing Five

pers. Sending a quick note to let someone know you are thinking of them, picking up some silly little thing that may mean a lot to someone, anonymously treating the person behind you in line, remembering what someone told you and asking about it later, acknowledging a difficulty and praying with someone through it, taking a moment to ask how someone is doing, meaning it, and actually giving them time to answer honestly, and so on. There are so many ways we can help others to feel God's love. It's trying to make sense of the why we have to do it that can stop us from acting on it. So don't ask "Why would I do that?" Just love – with action.

It's important to realize, though, that I can get overwhelmed if I think I must actively love everyone. God gifts me with specific appointments to certain people that He calls me to "love more." I try to pay attention enough to discern who they are. Some people are like a new bike at Christmas, easy to love. But let's face it, some can be like a hard fruitcake from my great aunt, a little tough to swallow. As a friend of mine said, "The people who are hardest to love are the ones who need love the most." I am always called to love, but with some people, I will be called to love more-with action. In any case, it doesn't matter how I "feel," I just need to "do." God is love, so everything He does represents it. He's the best teacher ever if we listen and follow.

God doesn't just hope I will love, He instructs me to. Make no mistake, He calls me to love and even refers to it in the two greatest commandments. First, we need to love Him, with action. What is it that God cares about the most? Me! Okay, and you! I love those shirts that say, "I'm God's Favorite," but I digress...back to love. Have you

---

♥ 1 John 4:8 NIV
4 Whoever does not love does not know God, because God is love.

🪨 Matthew 22:36-40 NIV
36 "Teacher, which is the greatest commandment in the Law?" 37 Jesus replied: "Love the Lord your God with all your heart and with all your soul and with all your mind.' 38 This is the first and greatest commandment. 39 And the second is like it: 'Love your neighbor as yourself.' 40 All the Law and the Prophets hang on these two commandments."

ever asked God how His day was (which is like a thousand years, so settle in), what incredible thing He did today, what you can do for Him today? Crazy, right? I know God doesn't need anything from me. I know that He can accomplish all things perfectly on His own. But wouldn't it just bless His heart if I asked? I'm pretty sure His answer would be something like, "It was an amazing day! So many people shared about My Son and entered the Kingdom. I was just parting seas and putting up hedges of protection around my children, and the like. I don't really need anything but thank you for asking. Oh by the way, I'm sending you on an incredible mission. You are going to have the best time ever. Now, what do you need, My child?"

Loving people isn't always easy. It can be a lot of work. I don't imagine it was very easy for God to love us when it meant sending His Son to die on a cross for our yuckiness, knowing we weren't really going to fully appreciate it, and some not at all. Because love is an action, it can also take sacrifice. Sometimes I'm going to have to let go of what I need in order to grab on to what someone else needs. There have been plenty of times in my life when I prayed for the wisdom and courage to love someone well. "Lord, please tell me how." Sometimes I succeed, sometimes I don't quite get there. But I assure you, I am always trying my best. Sometimes I must rely on the fact that God will do the loving for me if I miss the mark. When I don't have any of my own love, when I can't find what to do, I can always tap into God's love for them. I call it using my "Jesus Love," and I have used it on many occasions. We have all encountered people in our lives that aren't as easy to love, not because we don't have the feeling but because we don't

Thing Five

know the right way to "do" it. People are not easy, including myself, so I'm thankful when others use their Jesus love for me, too. He always knows the best way. I've discovered that it's much easier to love people if you see them as who God made them to be and not who the world has tricked them into being. That's how He sees me, and I'm so glad.

"THING SIX"

(Before reading this section, please see the Bible Study & Reflection for "Thing Six.")

> Romans 8:31 NKJV
> 31 What then shall we say to these things? If God is for us, who can be against us?

GOD IS FOR me, so He can't be against me. Since this is true, who else can be against me? No one! He is always working things for my good because I love Him and have been called according to His purpose (Romans 8:28). There is nothing that God does or allows that is intended by Him to harm me. Some things may be harmful, but that is the result of sin, mine and/or others. Still, any difficulty I face is intended to point me in the direction of the cross. Hardships are allowed by God to reveal my deep need for a Savior and His Grace and knowing my Savior Jesus is the only thing that affords me eternity in Heaven. That is the most important thing to Him, that I end up with Him for eternity.

There is nothing happening that our Lord and Savior has not already seen and prepared us for. It is so easy in

> John 14:6 NKJV
> 6 Jesus said to him, "I am the way, the truth, and the life. No one comes to the Father except through Me.

the hard times to become saddened and unsure of the future, but I need to remember that while this world is being moved by satan, the entire universe is being molded by God to accomplish His purpose. Silly satan, he doesn't know that even what he accomplishes is being used for God's glory. What a fun thing to think about when satan is messing with me. But often there's no need for satan's intervention in my life. I do a fine job of messing things up all on my own. And when I am, all he needs to do is glance my way and see that I'm doing his job for him. That is less fun to contemplate.

I was born into a stinky world that is full of good, but only because He fills it. We live in such a challenging time. Our world is at odds with itself, and we are at odds with each other. The news is reporting only the topics that sell, which isn't the "good, everything is going right" stuff, it's the "falling apart" stuff. I lose my ability to focus on all the good that God has going on if the only thing I ever see and hear is how messy the world is. It is ever so important to be continuously reminded that God is in control. He is on the throne and moving on behalf of each of us. We need to remember that regardless of the circumstances, He is going to show up and make it beautiful. I know that there are many situations where this is almost impossible to believe, but it's true! My job is to believe that. But how?

There is a story in the Bible (Mark 9:14-29) about a man who brought his sick child to the Lord to be healed. The disciples had already tried to cast out the demon that had a hold on the boy, so the father was less than optimistic. At the father's request, Jesus tells him that if he can believe, all things are possible to him who believes. The text

Thing Six

tells us that the man "immediately cried out and said with tears, "Lord, I believe; help my unbelief," and Jesus cast out the demon that afflicted the boy." Some versions say, "Lord, I believe, forgive my unbelief." The significance is the man was able to confess that he wasn't completely convinced that his boy would be healed. He lacked "big" faith, but he was sure that Jesus could fix that, too. And Jesus did.

God understands my humanness and inability to see Him at work in my darkest hours. He also understands that it can be difficult to remember to give Him ALL the glory when things go well. I have struggled with control issues and a spirit of pride that often convinces me that I've got it and really don't need God's help. Even then He is on my side...always working to put right what has gone wrong. As I move away, He follows. As I push away, He draws near. As I rebel, He showers me with grace, never keeping a record of wrong.

God loves me with every Fruit of His Spirit. He is for me, not against me. This is the example that I need to follow when reaching out to others. It's worth asking, "Does my life reflect love, joy, peace, patience, kindness, goodness, faithfulness, gentleness, and self-control?" 🍎 I try, and my life does demonstrate all of them at different times, but never all of them all the time. One day, everything will be right by His coming again, and all believers will be walking in the Spirit and all His Fruit continuously. Hallelujah! Until then, my faith lies in being sure of things hoped for, the evidence I can't yet see.♫ When my faith falls short, I can simply ask Him to forgive my unbelief and move on my behalf anyway, and He will! What He

---

🍎 Galatians 5:22-23 NKJV
22 But the fruit of the Spirit is love, joy, peace, longsuffering, kindness, goodness, faithfulness, 23 gentleness, self-control. Against such there is no law.

♫ Hebrews 1:11 NKJV
1 Now faith is the substance of things hoped for, the evidence of things not seen.

wants more than anything is for me to seek Him. I need to in the good times, bad times, easy times, hard times, all the time. When I do, the peace that passes my understanding fills my soul because God is for me. 🍎

🍎 Philippians 4:7 NKJV
7 …and the peace of God, which surpasses all understanding, will guard your hearts and minds through Christ Jesus.

"THING SEVEN"

(Before reading this section, please see the Bible Study & Reflection for "Thing Seven.")

SOME THINGS I just can't understand, and that is one of the hardest things. I was born with an inquisitive mind and am always seeking the "why" behind the "what." We are made in His image, but do our minds work the same? Maybe. But even if that is true, His mind is so much more advanced and capable. He's got a lot going on and if I try to understand it all, I get confused and overwhelmed with that desire to understand. Only He can make complete sense of things, and I need to be okay with that. It's not as hard now as it used to be. I've learned to trust that when I don't understand, He does.

When something doesn't make any sense at all, when it can't be explained but it is good and miraculous, then it is God. When something is difficult, horrible, and hard to

---

Genesis 1:27 NKJV
27 So God created man in His own image; in the image of God He created him; Male and female He created them.

go through, then it is the messy world we live in or a result of my own decisions and actions because of the world we live in. Either way, it may not be easy to understand. So many things are hard to understand. Why do bad things happen to good people? Why do children have to die? Why is there so much conflict in the world today? How does God hear everyone's prayers at the same time? There are so many questions that we, as humans, lack the ability to fully understand or answer. But the most accurate answer to every question is one or more of these...because God allowed it, sent it, is immeasurable, is all knowing, is love, is just, is omnipresent, omnipotent, omniscient, sovereign, transcendent...the list goes on. The shorter answer is because He knows best and is constantly moving on my behalf. God does not make bad things happen; sin does that. But He does allow difficulties sometimes to draw us near to Him. I've said it over and over...if everything were good all the time, then why would I need a Savior? It's in the most difficult times that I cry out to God. He longs to hear it, but I believe His heart hopes to one day hear it as often in the good times as when I need something. Either way, He is filled with joy when I turn to Him.

I'm convinced that there are truths that God has put in play just to remind us that we aren't big enough to perceive the reality, purpose, and/or result in every situation. The Truth of the Trinity is a good example. It is something that a lot of people discount or struggle with because of an inability to understand. The word "trinity" is not found in the Bible. It is a conceptual word that has been reverently "coined" to represent God as a whole, made up of three different persons...God the Father, God the Son, and God the Holy Spirit. There is really no way

Thing Seven

to explain how it is; I just have to believe that it is, and I do. There are implications in the Bible, plurals used by God when, if it were just one of them out there, He wouldn't have used them. There are places where Jesus is named by God as the "Word" (John 1:14). The Bible also tells us, "In the beginning, the Word was with God and the Word WAS God." (John 1:1) We know that God has a Spirit because the Bible tells us that "By this you know the Spirit of God... (I John 4:2a) But to explain how the three persons are the same God is more difficult. Each is unique, but collective in nature. We just have to believe that. The doctrine to support the Trinity is in the Bible. While it seems unexplainable, I believe God has provided simple little ways for me to attempt to understand, even though I never fully will. I remember as a newly devoted follower, the egg metaphor was very helpful to me. An egg is a whole egg, but it is made up of three separate parts: the shell, the yolk, and the whites. If you take one of those out, it will no longer be a whole egg. That's how God is... whole...three persons in one. Without one of the persons, He wouldn't be whole. I believe this to be true by the Holy Spirit that lives inside of me, not by my own understanding. (Proverbs 3:5-6)

The Bible tells us that we have been saved by grace through faith. Without the faith part, the grace is ineffective. We must believe and tell others that we do. Take heart though, we only need a little faith to overcome. Thank you, Lord! He knows our weakness and inability to understand His work in whole, so He gives us a lot of room and as many do-overs as we need. Thank you again, Lord! Does this mean it is okay to stay in the place where He found me? Nope! If I truly believe, I need to

---

Ephesians 2:8 NKJV
8 For by grace you have been saved through faith, and that not of yourselves; it is the gift of God, 9not of works, lest anyone should boast.

Matthew 17:20 NKJV
20 So Jesus said to them, "Because of your unbelief; for assuredly, I say to you, if you have faith as a mustard seed, you will say to this mountain, 'Move from here to there,' and it will move; and nothing will be impossible for you.

move closer to Him in my walk. When I do, my sin nature diminishes and my ability to be obedient grows, not because of anything I'm doing, but because of what He is doing in me. This concept is hard to understand, too. But I know it is true. I've lived it and seen it in so many others.

Lastly, there is one thing I can always do when I am confused and don't understand--PRAY! He has asked us to pray and ask for wisdom. If we do, He will give it to us freely. It may not be the wisdom we thought we would receive, but it will be the wisdom that we need. What? I know, I know...its confusing. But that is just how it works because He knows how far our minds can go and how far our hearts can follow. The most beautiful thing is that when I know the Creator of the universe intimately, then I can trust that even when I don't understand, He is moving for me. I don't have to know everything...what an epiphany. I don't have to understand everything because the God I serve is understanding for me and moving my life in ways I could never do on my own. When I have faith in this, then God's Will can reign in my life, and He can use me as He desires. If I stop to try and understand everything, then I waste a lot of time doing that instead of doing what He has planned for me to do. Yep, I've done that, too.

> James 1:5 NKJV
> 5 If any of you lacks wisdom, let him ask of God, who gives to all liberally and without reproach, and it will be given to him.

"WRAPPING IT UP"

(Before reading this section, please see the Bible Study & Reflection for "Wrapping It Up"*).*

I HOPE THAT you have enjoyed a bit of my journey in Christ. More than anything, I hope it has been helpful to you in discovering who you are in Christ and how much He loves you. It took me many years to come to all of this. My prayer is that you are getting it sooner. Let's put the "you" in each one of the 7 Things.

1. God is not mad at you! He loves you and wants to see you at peace and in His presence.
2. Your life is short and temporary. Don't waste a minute!
3. You can take the easy road or the hard road. You choose. In the end, salvation is still yours if you believe that Jesus Christ is the Lord and Savior of your life and that He died for your sins, but don't you want to avoid the ruts on the way?

4. Your relationship with God can be tangible and real. You just have to invest your time and put your heart into it.
5. True love is not a feeling, it is an action. This is perfectly true in God's love for you. Use the example.
6. God is for you, not against you. Rest in this peace.
7. Some things you just can't understand, so have faith in Him and His love for you, knowing that He is moving on your behalf even when you can't see it.

I am so thankful for God's grace, love, and the opportunity He has given me to share my experiences with you. While I do not profess to have grasped it all, I will shout from the rooftops that I love the One True God and He is working in my life every day. Why He chooses to use me in any situation, I will never understand...I am so broken without Him. But He surely has used me, and I'm thankful. I have made so many mistakes in my life, so many times I would like to turn back time and do it differently. While I cannot, I can still rest in His forgiveness, extend the same forgiveness to others, and do my best to listen to His voice the next time so I don't make the same mistake.

I can't wait to see what God has in store for today, tomorrow, and beyond. With God, and because of the miracle of the resurrection of Jesus Christ, there is no end to my story, only a new chapter each day and forever. Some days are harder than others. Most days are more amazing than I thought they could ever be. I'll take them both, knowing that I serve a God who is completely in control of it all. I don't always achieve it, but I work hard these days at choosing joy over frustration, sadness, and/or anger. If I truly believe what I have written for you here, I should be able

Wrapping It Up

to. Still, perfection is impossible in this life. But I will continue to trust that where I go, He will follow. Thanks for being a part of the reason that I've been reminded by the Father, Son, and Holy Spirit how much He loves me and how He is moving in me, around me, through me, and for me. God's richest blessings to you and those you care about.

BIBLE STUDY & REFLECTION

INTRODUCTION

Before reading the Introduction, read and reflect on the following –

Read I Corinthians 7:7

1. Is there something inside of you that God has been calling you to "let out?" (Journal your thoughts here.)
_____
_____
_____
_____
_____.

2. What is one gift that you know you have but that you have yet to start using, or have used but not so much anymore, for God's glory.
_____
_____
_____
_____
_____.

3. Give some examples of emotions and beliefs that can keep you from moving forward in God's good and perfect Will for your life.

_____
_____
_____
_____
_____.

Read the Introduction.

1. Do *you* believe in you…like God believes in you? Reflect on this and journal your thoughts.

_____
_____
_____
_____.
_____
_____
_____
_____
_____.
_____
_____
_____
_____.

WHY "7" THINGS?

Before reading Why "7" Things, read and reflect on the following –

1. Do you have a God story? If yes, what is it? (Continue on a separate sheet if needed.)
　_____
　_____
　_____
　_____
　_____.

2. Do you think it is important to share your God story with others? Why or why not?
　_____
　_____
　_____
　_____.

3. Give your own definition of "mentor."
_____
_____
_____
_____
_____.

4. Who are your mentors and sisters/brothers?
_____
_____
_____
_____
_____.

5. Who are your sisters/brothers and friends?
_____
_____
_____
_____
_____.

6. Who are the people in your life that God has called you to mentor?
_____
_____
_____
_____
_____.

7. Can you see yourself in your life today in all three of these identities? (Detail which you do and/or do not, and reflect the "why" of it.)

_____
_____
_____
_____
_____.

Read Psalms 145:4, II Timothy 2:2, and Proverbs 27:17

1. How do these verses from God's Word apply to your answers above? Have your answers changed?

_____
_____
_____
_____
_____.

"THING ONE"

God is not mad at me, and His love is unconditional!

<u>Before</u> reading "Thing One", read and reflect on the following –

1. Have you ever struggled with feelings of unworthiness or that you aren't good enough for God? Explain.
_____
_____
_____
_____
_____.

2. How do you imagine that God sees you?
_____
_____
_____
_____
_____.

3. How do you imagine God reacts when we "misbehave" or sin?

_____
_____
_____
_____
_____.

4. How many of your sins are sins that you would commit after Jesus died on the cross for you? (Hint – Jesus died about 2000 years ago.)

_____
_____
_____
_____
_____.

5. If you know and love Jesus, does that mean you should be able to be perfect all the time?

_____
_____
_____
_____
_____.

Read "Thing One" and the following scriptures:

Romans 5:1, Romans 8:1, 1 John 1:9, Romans 8:28-30, 2 Corinthians 5:16-21

Bible Study & Reflection

2. How do these verses from God's Word apply to your answers above? Have your answers changed?

"THING TWO"

This life is short and temporary by God's design.

Before reading "Thing Two," read and reflect on the following –

1. List some circumstances you have encountered in your life that are/were difficult and made this life seem long and hard.
_____
_____
_____
_____
_____.

2. In tough circumstances, where do you find yourself looking? Are you focused on the issue or the victory in it?
_____
_____
_____
_____
_____.

3. Do you believe God causes bad things to happen? Yes or no, and why?

_____
_____
_____
_____
_____.

4. Why do you think bad things happen?

_____
_____
_____
_____
_____.

5. Give your definition of joy, then give your definition of happiness. Do you see them the same?

_____
_____
_____
_____
_____.

6. Do you believe in and allow yourself to imagine your "forever" in Heaven? Tell about it.

_____
_____
_____
_____
_____.

Bible Study & Reflection

Read "Thing Two" and the following scriptures:
John 16:33, II Corinthians 4:17-18, I John 5:11, 1 Corinthians 6:3, Job 20 4-5

1. How do these verses from God's Word apply to your answers above? Have your answers changed?

"THING THREE"
I can take the hard road or the easy road.

<u>Before</u> reading "Thing Three," read and reflect on the following –

1. Do you feel as if a good portion of this life is spent in struggle? Explain.
_____
_____
_____
_____
_____.

2. How often do you think the struggle is a result of your own choices? How often do you think they are the result of someone else's choices? Give some examples to explore.
_____
_____
_____
_____
_____.

3. As a child of God, how important are the choices we make? Why?

_____
_____
_____
_____
_____.

4. Contemplate and give your understanding of the word "discipline." When do we need it? When do we impose it on our children or others under our authority?

_____
_____
_____
_____
_____.

5. Do you generally find yourself asking God for direction ahead of time or, more often rescue after the fact?

_____
_____
_____
_____
_____.

6. Are you on the easy road or the hard road? How can you be sure?

_____
_____
_____
_____
_____.

Bible Study & Reflection

Read "Thing Three" and the following scriptures:

Hebrews 12:4-13, Proverbs 3:1-6, Romans 3:23-24, 1 John 1:9, Matthew 7:13-14

1. How do these verses from God's Word apply to your answers above? Have your answers changed?

_____
_____
_____
_____
_____
_____
_____
_____
_____
_____
_____
_____
_____
_____
_____
_____
_____
_____
_____
_____
_____
_____
_____.

"THING FOUR"

Relationship with God is tangible and real.

Before reading "Thing Four," read and reflect on the following –

1. Describe the characteristics of a healthy relationship.
   _____
   _____
   _____
   _____.

2. Do you believe that you can have a real and tangible relationship with God? If yes, how do you experience it?
   _____
   _____
   _____
   _____.

3. Do you believe God wants to have a close relationship with you? Why or why not?

_____
_____
_____
_____
_____.

4. How does God speak to you? Have you heard His voice?

_____
_____
_____
_____
_____.

5. How do you speak to God? Do you believe He hears your every word?

_____
_____
_____
_____
_____.

Read "Thing Four" and the following scriptures:

Luke 20:38, Ephesians 5:29-32, John 1:18, 1 John 4:7-10, Matthew 6:6, Proverbs 7:1-2

6. What steps can we take to enter into a more intimate relationship with God?

"THING FIVE"

True love is not a feeling, it's an action.

<u>Before</u> reading "Thing Five," read and reflect on the following –

1. What does the word "love" mean to you? Can you define it?
_____
_____
_____
_____.

2. How do you know if someone genuinely "loves" you?
_____
_____
_____
_____
_____.

3. If we "love" someone, what does that look like?
_____
_____
_____
_____
_____.

4. Is love sometimes difficult? Why or why not?
_____
_____
_____
_____
_____.

5. Do you see yourself as easy to love?
_____
_____
_____
_____
_____.

Read "Thing Five" and the following scriptures:

John 3:16, Romans 5:8, Luke 6:35, 1 John 4:19, 2 John 1:6, Romans 8:37-39

Bible Study & Reflection

1. What does God's Word speak to your heart about love? What steps can we take to enter into a more intimate relationship with God and others?

"THING SIX"

God is for me, so He can't be against me.

<u>Before</u> reading "Thing Six," read and reflect on the following –

1. Who is your greatest fan, the person in your life that encourages you in all your endeavors? Describe that person.
   _____
   _____
   _____
   _____
   _____ .

2. Do you believe that God is ALWAYS on your side?
   _____
   _____
   _____
   _____
   _____ .

3. Are there people in your life that seem to be against you?
_____
_____
_____
_____.

4. Are you sure they are, or could it be your perspective? (This is not a trick question. Answer as honestly as you can.)
_____
_____
_____
_____.

5. When you look at the world today, can you see good? Is the world around you trying to remind you of the good or the bad going on today?
_____
_____
_____
_____.

Read "Thing Six" and the following scriptures:

Luke 12:4-5, Romans 8:28, Ephesians 6:12, 1 John 2:16-17, 2 Corinthians 7:10, Philippians 4:5-6

1. How do these verses from God's Word apply to your answers above? How can we be reminded of the good going on around us?

"THING SEVEN"

*Some things I just can't understand and
that is one of the hardest things.*

<u>Before</u> reading "Thing Seven," read and reflect on the following –

1. What circumstances in your life do you find yourself struggling to understand to no avail?
_____
_____
_____
_____.

2. Do you find yourself asking "why" things happen and becoming frustrated when you can't find the answer?
_____
_____
_____
_____.

3. Define "faith" in your own words.

_____
_____
_____
_____.

4. Do you believe God is working on your behalf even in the moments that you don't see or understand that He is? Explain your answer.

_____
_____
_____
_____.

5. How can we find peace in our inability to understand what God is up to?

_____
_____
_____
_____.

Read "Thing Seven" and the following scriptures:

Ecclesiastes 11:5, Proverbs 3:5-6, Luke 24:44-45, Matthew 15:10

Bible Study & Reflection

1. God wants us to understand what we are able but protects us from what we are not yet prepared to understand. As we grow in our relationship, we are able to understand more. Describe how this speaks to your heart.

"WRAPPING IT UP"

Read "Wrapping It Up" and describe in detail how one of the "Seven Things" has resonated in your heart and inspired you to grow closer to the One True God who created you and loves you unconditionally.

_____
_____
_____
_____
_____
_____
_____
_____
_____
_____
_____
_____
_____
_____

SPECIAL THANKS

I'D LIKE TO take a minute to extend a sincere thank you to those who were committed to helping me get this project completed. Firstly, thank you Lord for inspiring my heart to write. I stand in awe that You would use little 'ol me. To my amazing husband, Jerry, you have held my arms up so many times that I've lost count. Thank you for your tireless grace, encouragement, and love. Not surprisingly because of the God we serve, you are more than I could have asked for or imagined and I am abundantly blessed by your presence in my life every day. To my sissy, Sandy, I love you more than you can know and am so thankful for your amazing ability to edit and see things that others don't. Your heart for God is an inspiration and I'm so blessed to call you my "sissy!" Thank you for your thorough review of this project and all the corrections and suggestions that made it what it is today. You are a blessing to me in so many ways. To my dear sisters in Christ who took the time to read this project and offer how the words impacted you and your spiritual journey. Amanda, Amy, Holly, Katie, Keshia, Linette, and Shorty, this book would not be what it is today without your input. Thank you for sharing your hearts with me. I can't wait to continue sharing our Jesus and God's rich, amazing plan for our lives. I see Jesus dancing over each one of you and pray all of His richest blessings in your lives. You are all my people, and I am ultimately blessed by your involvement with this project and in every way. Woot, woot…riding the Jesus train together. So honored!

ABOUT THE AUTHOR

JULIE HICKS is an up-and-coming writer who is passionate about family, music, and spreading the healing and redemptive power of Jesus. While her writing career is just kicking off with this first book and Bible Study Guide, she has always enjoyed sharing her gift with others in personal poetry and other forms of meaningful written expression to those experiencing joy, victory, loss, struggle, and difficulty in this life. Julie's hope is that everyone her writings touch will be drawn closer to a loving God who deeply desires a personal relationship with each one of us. Julie is the mother of three grown boys and lives with her husband in beautiful Colorado. In her spare time she enjoys singing with her church praise & worship group, planting and yard work, camping, riding ATVs, kayaking, and generally being outside in the beauty God has created around us. She also loves animals and currently volunteers at a local wildlife rehabilitation center. Julie is a hobby breeder bringing little bundles of dachshund love to her community and beyond.

Stop human trafficking!

www.ingramcontent.com/pod-product-compliance
Lightning Source LLC
LaVergne TN
LVHW062244070526
838201LV00093B/172